Published by Collins
An imprint of HarperCollins Publishers
HarperCollins Publishers
Westerhill Road
Bishopbriggs
Glasgow G64 2QT

www.harpercollins.co.uk

HarperCollins Publishers
1st Floor, Watermarque Building
Ringsend Road
Dublin 4, Ireland

10 9 8 7 6 5 4 3 2 1

All puzzles supplied by Clarity Media Ltd
All images © Shutterstock.com

ISBN 978-0-00-850340-6

Printed and bound in the UK using 100% renewable electricity at CPI Group (UK) Ltd

A catalogue record for this book is available from the British Library.

Publisher: Michelle I'Anson
Project Manager: Sarah Woods
Designer: Kevin Robbins

MIX
Paper from
responsible sources
FSC™ C007454

With more than 120 fun puzzles. you'll
never want to put this book down!

You can do them in any order. but they get harder as
you go through the book so you may wish to start
at the front and work through to the end.

See if you have got them right by checking
out the answers at the back of the book.

There are some blank pages too. which are
handy for jotting down workings. notes.
scribbles or whatever you like!

So... are you ready to

FOLDED PAPER

COUNTRY

MOUNTAIN

BIRTHDAY

Three pieces of paper have been folded in half. They each have a word on - can you work out what those words are?

4

WORDSPOT

A	P	A	P	A	P
P	A	L	A	A	E
P	L	E	P	A	A
L	L	P	P	L	E
P	A	L	L	L	P
E	P	A	E	P	L

Find the word 'apple' in the grid. It may be hidden horizontally, vertically or diagonally.

WORD LADDER

BIKE

LIKE

RAMP

Move from the word at the top of the ladder to the word at the bottom of the ladder by changing one letter on each step of the ladder to form a new word. Do not rearrange the order of the letters.

MISSING VOWELS

SWMMNG

TRVLLNG

CLCLTR

GHTN

MRTHN

MBRLL

These six words have had their vowels removed. Can you add them back in to find the words?

WORDFINDER

G	A	M
V	V	I
I	V	E

A word has been hidden in the letter grid above. Simply cross out any letter that appears more than once and the hidden word will reveal itself. If you'd like an added challenge, see if you can solve the puzzle in your head without crossing any letters out.

WORD ILLUSION

SASW

HA8D

RÆKÆL

Pairs of words have been superimposed on top of each other. Can you work out what the words are?

BREAK THE CODE

QBQFS =

DSBZPO =

SVMFS =

Each of these stationery items has had each letter replaced by the letter before it in the alphabet (so 'B' becomes 'A' and so on). Can you break the code to reveal the answers?

WORDWHEEL

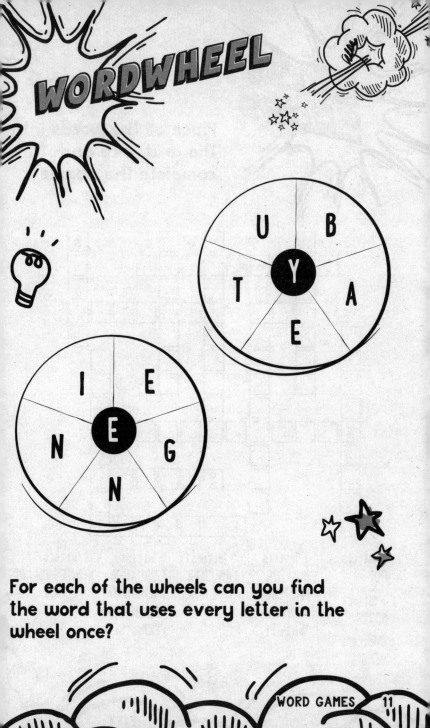

For each of the wheels can you find the word that uses every letter in the wheel once?

KRISS KROSS

Place all the words into the grid once each to complete the puzzle.

3 letters
PUG

5 letters
BOXER

6 letters
BEAGLE

7 letters
BULLDOG
MALTESE
POINTER
WHIPPET

8 letters
LANDSEER

9 letters
CHIHUAHUA
DALMATIAN
GREYHOUND
PEKINGESE

12 letters
NEWFOUNDLAND

WORD SPLITS

ETY SAF

EMA CIN

TER EAS

These three words have been split into smaller sections and shuffled around. Can you put them back in order?

CODEBREAKER

Carefully and slowly read this sentence and little by little the answer to this moderately quick puzzle should reveal itself.

Can you find the additional word concealed in this sentence above?

ANAGRAM CONNECT

Follow the line from each letter at the top and write that letter in the empty circle it is connected to. These letters will spell out the answer word.

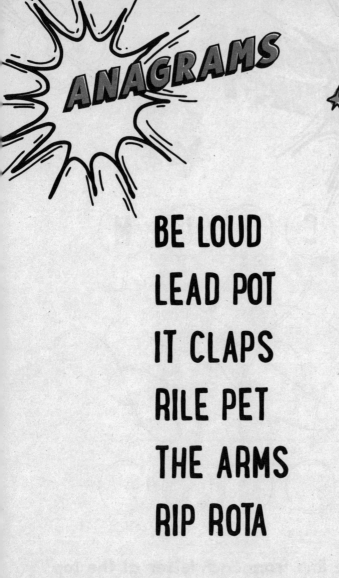

ANAGRAMS

BE LOUD

LEAD POT

IT CLAPS

RILE PET

THE ARMS

RIP ROTA

Can you rearrange the scrambled letters to reveal six new words?

FOLDED PAPER

PATIENT

CREATIVE

ADDITION

Three pieces of paper have been folded in half. They each have a word on - can you work out what those words are?

WORDWHEEL

For each of the wheels can you find the word that uses every letter in the wheel once?

WORDFINDER

C	H	A
K	H	E
S	S	S

A word has been hidden in the letter grid above. Simply cross out any letter that appears more than once and the hidden word will reveal itself. If you'd like an added challenge, see if you can solve the puzzle in your head without crossing any letters out.

WORDSEARCH

Find each of the words in the grid. Words may be hidden horizontally or vertically.

```
P T L A U G H T E R A D
L P B A L L O O N S F R
F A M I L Y P B W X J I
F C E L E B R A T I O N
R C A N D L E S K C M K
I Z R Y B A S V F A U S
E A K L H I E C O K S H
N D A N C I N G O E I I
D T O X S P T R D R C O
S Z A S Z U S G A M E S
O L G S U R P R I S E R
P A R T Y H A T S S F G
```

BALLOONS   DRINKS   LAUGHTER
CAKE   FAMILY   MUSIC
CANDLES   FOOD   PARTY HATS
CELEBRATION   FRIENDS   PRESENTS
DANCING   GAMES   SURPRISE

WORD LADDER

READ

BEAD

BOOK

Move from the word at the top of the ladder to the word at the bottom of the ladder by changing one letter on each step of the ladder to form a new word. Do not rearrange the order of the letters.

WORDFINDER

E	H	T
H	E	H
U	N	A

A word has been hidden in the letter grid above. Simply cross out any letter that appears more than once and the hidden word will reveal itself. If you'd like an added challenge, see if you can solve the puzzle in your head without crossing any letters out.

?ADNES?

?CLIPS?

?OMI?

?EGISTE?

?NTRANC?

?ALEN?

On each of these words the same letter has been removed from the start and end, and replaced with a question mark. The missing letters all spell out a word, can you work out what it is?

WORD SPLITS

ABLE TIMET

CING DAN

TLE CAS

These three words have been split into smaller sections and shuffled around. Can you put them back in order?

CROSSWORD

Across

1 Planet that is reddish in colour (4)
3 Someone you look up to (4)
5 Your way of writing your name (9)
6 Costly (9)
8 Not right (9)
10 Bright object in the sky (4)
11 Opposite of minus (4)

Down

1 Unexplained things (9)
2 E.g. touch or smell (5)
3 Warm (3)
4 These are made from beaten eggs cooked in frying pans (9)
7 Sticky liquid put on a pancake (5)
9 Item used to move a rowing boat (3)

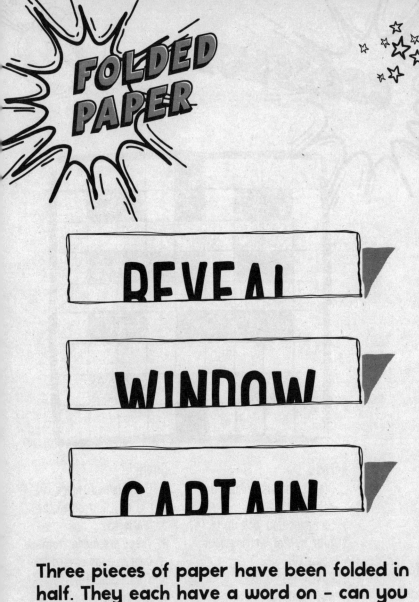

FOLDED PAPER

REVEAL

WINDOW

CAPTAIN

Three pieces of paper have been folded in half. They each have a word on - can you work out what those words are?

ANAGRAM CONNECT

Follow the line from each letter at the top and write that letter in the empty circle it is connected to. These letters will spell out the answer word.

MISSING VOWELS

NVRNMNT

WNDRFL

DGHNT

CMDN

MTRBK

NNSNS

These six words have had their vowels removed. Can you add them back in to find the words?

WORDWHEEL

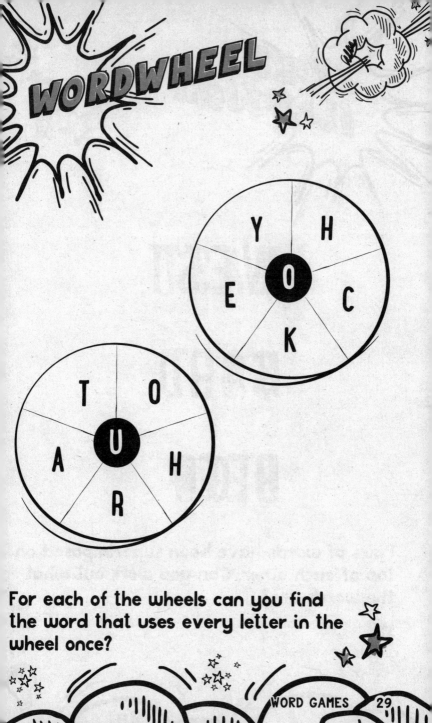

For each of the wheels can you find the word that uses every letter in the wheel once?

WORD ILLUSION

WÆST

BARD

BEGR

Pairs of words have been superimposed on top of each other. Can you work out what the words are?

BREAK THE CODE

PSBOHF =

QVSQMF =

ZFMMPX =

Each of these colours has had each letter replaced by the letter before it in the alphabet (so 'B' becomes 'A' and so on). Can you break the code to reveal the answers?

CODEBREAKER

Andy and Rebecca were on thir way to school and were discussing their favourite subjects. Andy metioned that he loved history more than any other subject, whilst Rebecca said she loved learning lanuages, and particulary Spanish, which was her favourite subject. If you crack ths code, you'll succesfully reveal the name of another scool subject.

Read the above paragraph of text carefully and see if you can work out how the code works to find the answer word.

WORDSPOT

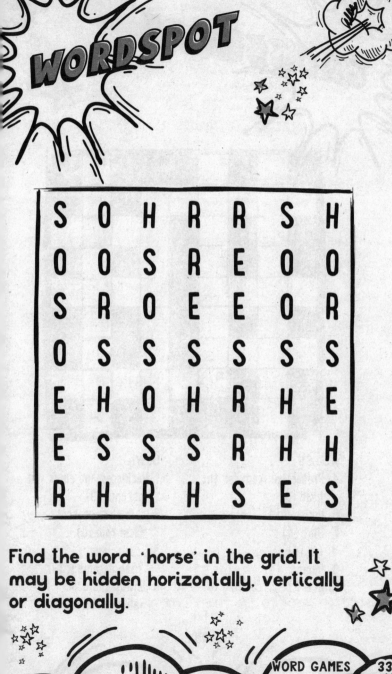

S	O	H	R	R	S	H
O	O	S	R	R	O	O
S	R	O	E	E	O	R
O	S	S	S	S	S	S
E	H	O	H	R	H	E
E	S	S	S	R	H	H
R	H	R	H	S	E	S

Find the word 'horse' in the grid. It may be hidden horizontally, vertically or diagonally.

CROSSWORD

Across
4 Protective item for the head (6)
6 Unusual (4)
7 Hint (4)
8 Too (4)
9 Genuine (4)
10 In a foreign country (6)

Down
1 Necklaces and rings, for instance (9)
2 Item that protects you from rain (8)
3 ＿＿＿ Day: 25th December (9)
5 Jewels and other valuable items (8)

WORDFINDER

S	L	L	Y
S	E	A	N
J	W	W	C
R	N	J	C

A word has been hidden in the letter grid above. Simply cross out any letter that appears more than once and the hidden word will reveal itself. If you'd like an added challenge, see if you can solve the puzzle in your head without crossing any letters out.

WORD LADDER

BIRD
BIND

NEST

Move from the word at the top of the ladder to the word at the bottom of the ladder by changing one letter on each step of the ladder to form a new word. Do not rearrange the order of the letters.

36

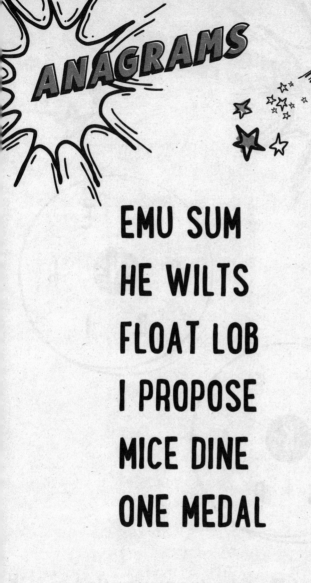

ANAGRAMS

EMU SUM

HE WILTS

FLOAT LOB

I PROPOSE

MICE DINE

ONE MEDAL

Can you rearrange the scrambled letters to reveal six new words?

WORDWHEEL

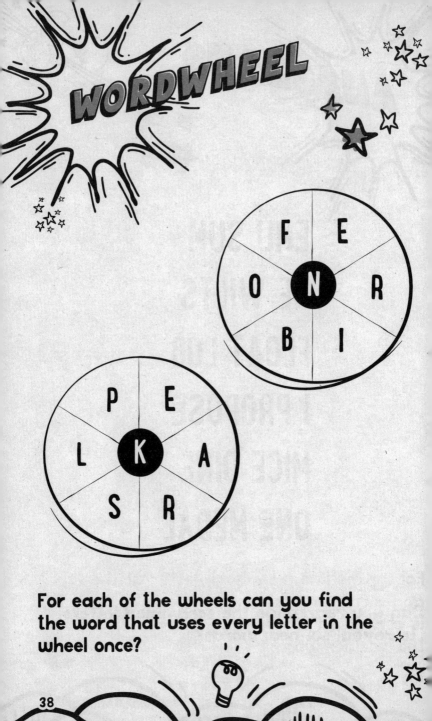

For each of the wheels can you find the word that uses every letter in the wheel once?

ANAGRAM CONNECT

Follow the line from each letter at the top and write that letter in the empty circle it is connected to. These letters will spell out the answer word.

WORDSEARCH

Find each of the words in the grid. Words may be hidden horizontally or vertically.

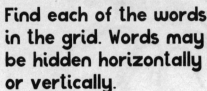

```
M  O  N  G  O  L  I  A  P  S  I  A
C  H  I  N  A  I  N  D  I  A  T  R
T  I  Z  C  U  N  E  B  P  J  T  G
W  A  E  P  S  D  Z  R  O  A  E  E
U  M  U  O  T  O  L  A  L  P  R  N
I  Z  I  R  R  N  U  Z  A  A  J  T
E  I  N  T  A  E  F  I  N  N  M  I
A  T  L  U  L  S  P  L  D  X  Z  N
E  A  V  G  I  I  C  A  N  A  D  A
P  L  E  A  A  A  M  E  X  I  C  O
J  Y  T  L  S  R  U  S  S  I  A  T
B  W  A  L  G  E  R  I  A  E  O  Z
```

ALGERIA	CHINA	MEXICO
ARGENTINA	INDIA	MONGOLIA
AUSTRALIA	INDONESIA	POLAND
BRAZIL	ITALY	PORTUGAL
CANADA	JAPAN	RUSSIA

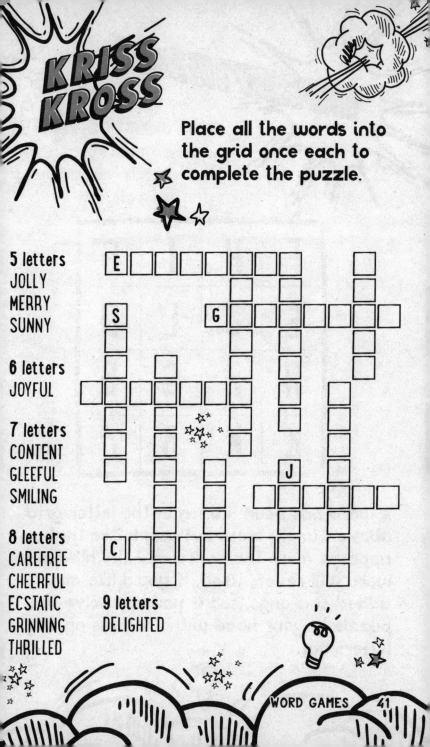

KRISS KROSS

Place all the words into the grid once each to complete the puzzle.

5 letters
JOLLY
MERRY
SUNNY

6 letters
JOYFUL

7 letters
CONTENT
GLEEFUL
SMILING

8 letters
CAREFREE
CHEERFUL
ECSTATIC
GRINNING
THRILLED

9 letters
DELIGHTED

WORDFINDER

F	H	I	G
E	J	L	D
H	B	G	B
K	K	B	J

A word has been hidden in the letter grid above. Simply cross out any letter that appears more than once and the hidden word will reveal itself. If you'd like an added challenge, see if you can solve the puzzle in your head without crossing any letters out.

BREAK THE CODE

SRPRSNGLY T S PSSBL FR TH HMN BRN T WRK T TH CNTNTS F SNTNCS VN WHN LL TH VWLS HV BN RMVD FRM THM. S Y HV JST DMNSTRTD.

Can you work out what this sentence says? Some letters have been removed from it.

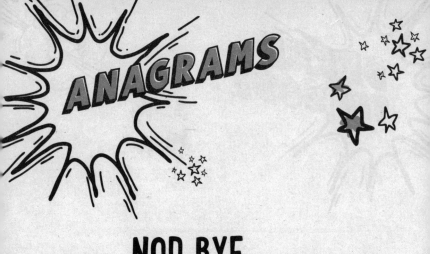

ANAGRAMS

NOD BYE

LOST KNEE

WOLF SNAKE

GREEN SPAS

EMU BRAINS

EYED TRAYS

Can you rearrange the scrambled letters to reveal six new words?

FOLDED PAPER

TICKET

ADVENTURE

DRAWING

Three pieces of paper have been folded in half. They each have a word on - can you work out what those words are?

ANAGRAM CONNECT

Follow the line from each letter at the top and write that letter in the empty circle it is connected to. These letters will spell out the answer word.

WORD SPLITS

ATE ANIM

ITY GRAV

FECT PER

These three words have been split into smaller sections and shuffled around. Can you put them back in order?

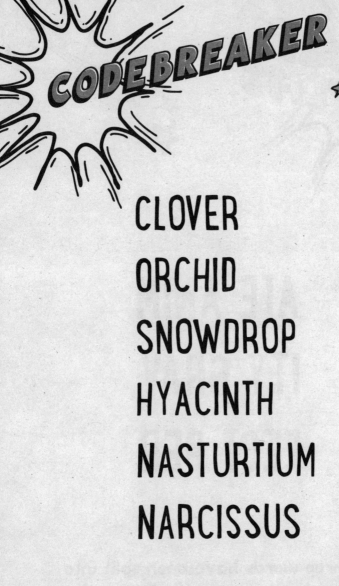

CODEBREAKER

CLOVER

ORCHID

SNOWDROP

HYACINTH

NASTURTIUM

NARCISSUS

Can you find the name of another flower hidden in the list above?

WORDWHEEL

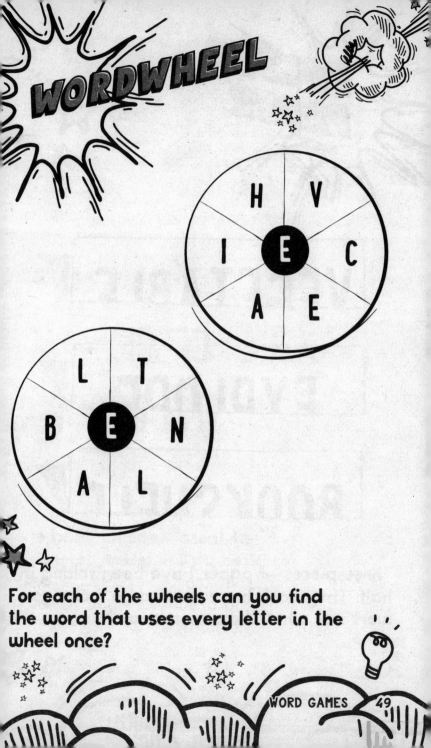

For each of the wheels can you find the word that uses every letter in the wheel once?

FOLDED PAPER

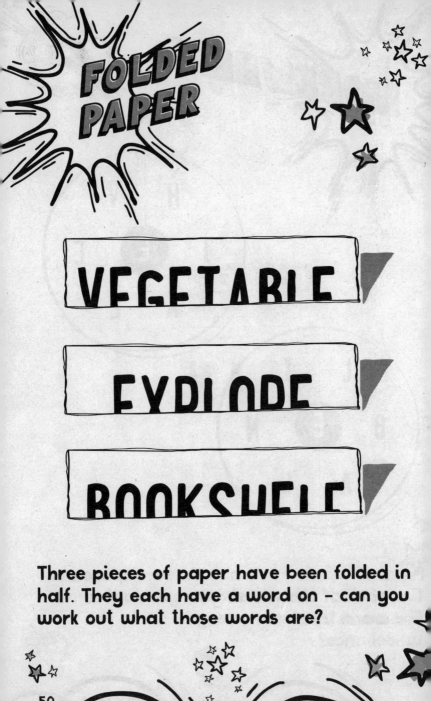

VEGETABLE

EXPLODE

BOOKSHELF

Three pieces of paper have been folded in half. They each have a word on - can you work out what those words are?

WORD ILLUSION

Pairs of words have been superimposed on top of each other. Can you work out what the words are?

CROSSWORD

Across

1 Chewy type of sweet (6)
6 E.g. Monopoly or Cluedo (5.4)
7 Broad smile (4)
8 Someone who does not tell the truth (4)
9 Country in South America (9)
11 Ten plus ten (6)

Down

1 Sledge (8)
2 Pink wading bird (8)
3 Finish (3)
4 Wizard (8)
5 Second month of the year (8)
10 Opposite of old (3)

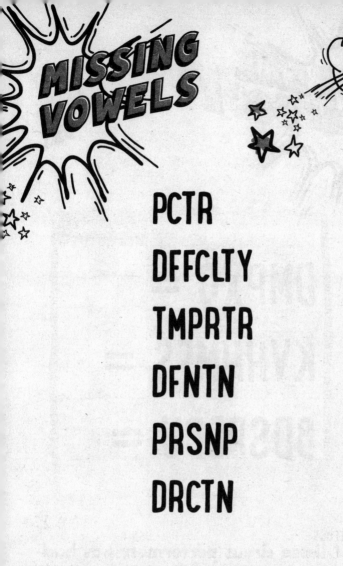

MISSING VOWELS

PCTR

DFFCLTY

TMPRTR

DFNTN

PRSNP

DRCTN

These six words have had their vowels removed. Can you add them back in to find the words?

BREAK THE CODE

$$DMPXO =$$

$$KVHHMFS =$$

$$BDSPCBU =$$

Each of these circus performers has had each letter replaced by the letter before it in the alphabet (so 'B' becomes 'A' and so on). Can you break the code to reveal the answers?

WORDFINDER

A word has been hidden in the letter grid above. Simply cross out any letter that appears more than once and the hidden word will reveal itself. If you'd like an added challenge, see if you can solve the puzzle in your head without crossing any letters out.

WORDWHEEL

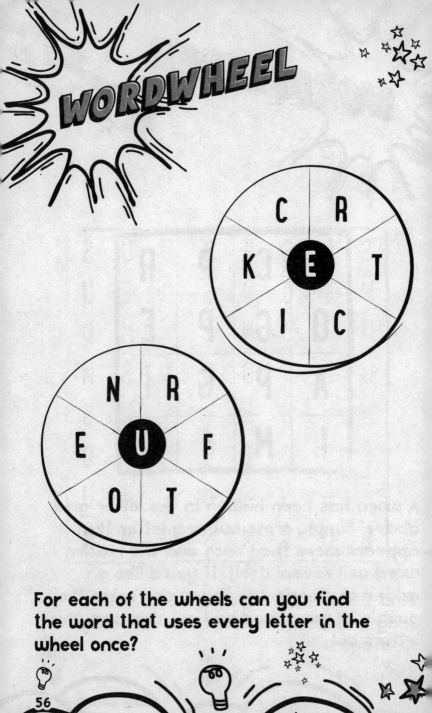

For each of the wheels can you find the word that uses every letter in the wheel once?

WORDSPOT

S	U	S	E	S	U	U	S
M	E	O	U	S	O	E	U
U	M	S	M	E	M	M	O
U	O	S	O	U	S	S	M
M	U	S	E	U	S	U	S
S	S	O	E	O	M	M	O
E	E	S	E	O	E	M	U
E	U	S	M	S	O	M	M

Find the word 'mouse' in the grid. It may be hidden horizontally, vertically or diagonally.

WORD SPLITS

PA SS COM

ARK SP LE

WE ND EKE

These three words have been split into smaller sections and shuffled around. Can you put them back in order?

BREAK THE CODE

My first is in banana and in pear
My second is in peek but not in stare
My third is the middle letter of compare
My fourth is in triangle but not in square
My fifth is not in rabbit but is in hare

Can you solve this riddle to reveal the name of a fruit?

WORDSEARCH

Find each of the words in the grid. Words may be hidden horizontally, vertically or diagonally.

```
S P N I U U S U P M L E H
F B U D G E R I G A R T P
I S D Y T O L Z F L A R I
S Z F S D A J I D R N O G
H S O P K H R L Z O O A Y
S R R A C P A A O A G G D
G A A T S A S M N J R F P
E B S U N R T F S T C D S
R B V R A R I E S T U P L
B I A T K O L R O H E L R
I T E L E T W R E B U R A
L W N E Q R E E K H A O S
S L B Q A R J T G S I E L
```

BUDGERIGAR	FROG	PIG
CAT	GERBIL	RABBIT
DOG	HAMSTER	SNAKE
FERRET	LIZARD	TARANTULA
FISH	PARROT	TURTLE

WORD ILLUSION

GOAD / GOOD / TOAD

ADULT / ABOUT / ...

ABOVE / ALCOVE / ...

Pairs of words have been superimposed on top of each other. Can you work out what the words are?

FOLDED PAPER

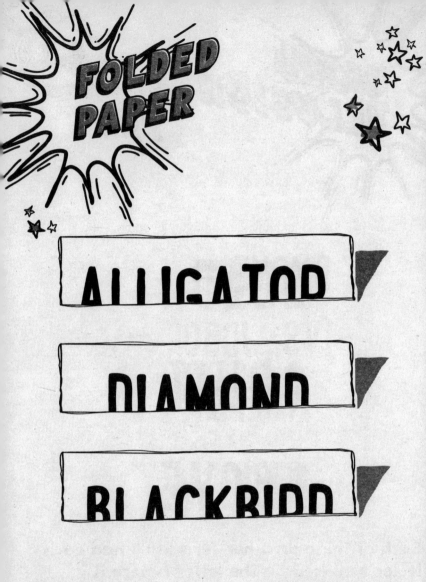

ALLIGATOR

DIAMOND

BLACKBIRD

Three pieces of paper have been folded in half. They each have a word on – can you work out what those words are?

BREAK THE CODE

DMPVE =

IVSSJDBOF =

UIVOEFS =

Each of these weather terms has had each letter replaced by the letter before it in the alphabet (so 'B' becomes 'A' and so on). Can you break the code to reveal the answers?

MISSING VOWELS

PRCPN

MRMLD

SMTMS

CCMBR

FRTNGHT

WRDRB

These six words have had their vowels removed. Can you add them back in to find the words?

64

WORDFINDER

L	Y	L	Y	C
J	H	S	B	H
X	R	J	C	E
U	G	U	I	I
X	A	S	D	G

A word has been hidden in the letter grid above. Simply cross out any letter that appears more than once and the hidden word will reveal itself. If you'd like an added challenge, see if you can solve the puzzle in your head without crossing any letters out.

ANAGRAM CONNECT

Follow the line from each letter at the top and write that letter in the empty circle it is connected to. These letters will spell out the answer word.

WORD LADDER

SNOW

FORT

Move from the word at the top of the ladder to the word at the bottom of the ladder by changing one letter on each step of the ladder to form a new word. Do not rearrange the order of the letters.

(Note: there may be more than one way to solve the puzzle. Word ladders often have multiple solutions.)

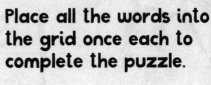

KRISS KROSS

Place all the words into the grid once each to complete the puzzle.

4 letters
DILL
SAGE

5 letters
BASIL
CUMIN
THYME

6 letters
CHIVES
GINGER
PEPPER

7 letters
OREGANO
PAPRIKA
PARSLEY

8 letters
ROSEMARY
TARRAGON

9 letters
CORIANDER

11 letters
HORSERADISH

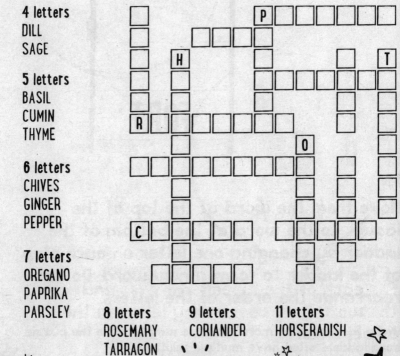

WORDWHEEL

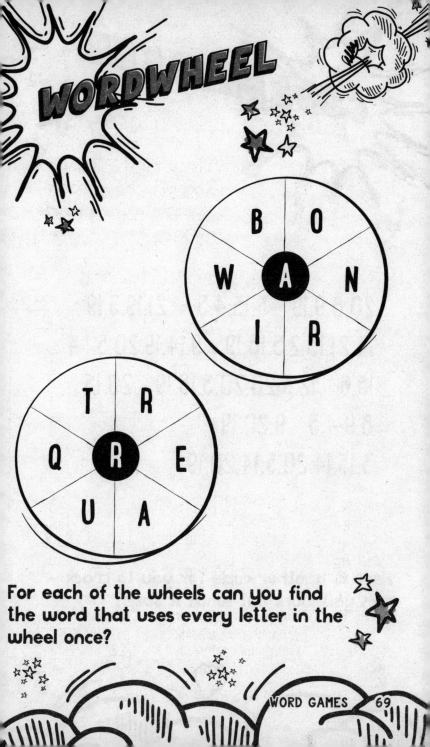

For each of the wheels can you find the word that uses every letter in the wheel once?

CODEBREAKER

20,8,9,19   3,15,4,5   21,19,5,19

14,21,13,2,5,18,19   9,14,19,20,5,1,4

15,6   12,5,20,20,5,18,19   20,15

8,9,4,5   9,20,19

3,15,14,20,5,14,20,19

Here is another code for you to crack – can you work out what it says?

70

WORD SPLITS

NIT URE FUR

ING AD RE

AKF BRE AST

These three words have been split into smaller sections and shuffled around. Can you put them back in order?

WORDFINDER

C	N	Z	G	N
B	O	F	E	I
L	I	Z	G	A
O	S	C	L	S
B	R	T	F	H

A word has been hidden in the letter grid above. Simply cross out any letter that appears more than once and the hidden word will reveal itself. If you'd like an added challenge, see if you can solve the puzzle in your head without crossing any letters out.

ANAGRAM CONNECT

Follow the line from each letter at the top and write that letter in the empty circle it is connected to. These letters will spell out the answer word.

WORDWHEEL

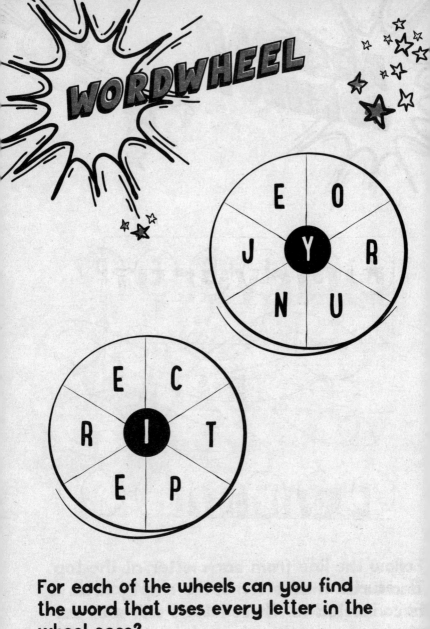

For each of the wheels can you find the word that uses every letter in the wheel once?

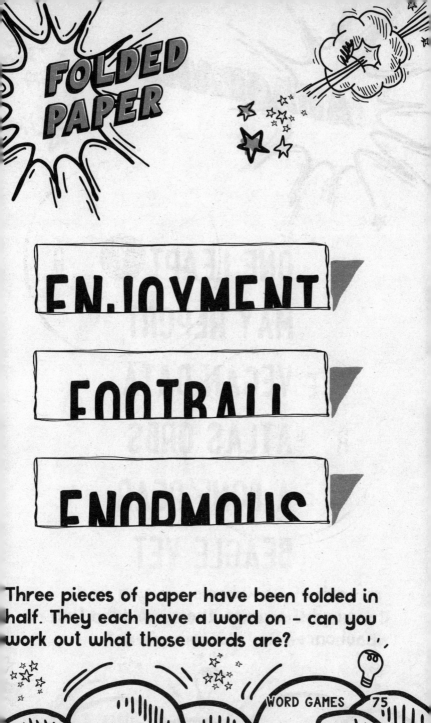

FOLDED PAPER

ENJOYMENT

FOOTBALL

ENORMOUS

Three pieces of paper have been folded in half. They each have a word on - can you work out what those words are?

ANAGRAMS

ONE LEAPT

MAY REPORT

VEGAN DATA

ATLAS ORBS

A LONE PEAR

BEAGLE VET

Can you rearrange the scrambled letters above to reveal six new words?

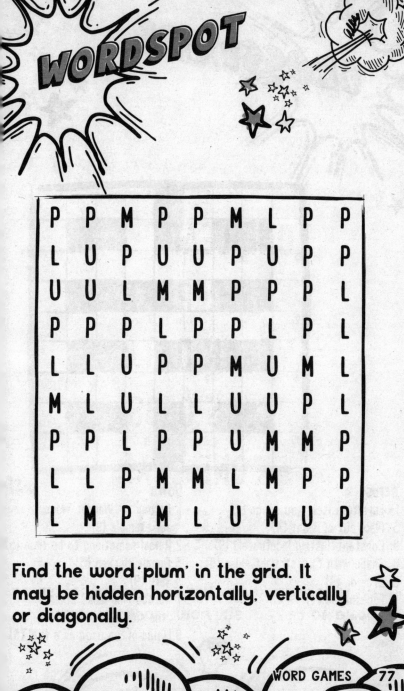

WORDSPOT

P	P	M	P	P	M	L	P	P
L	U	P	U	U	P	U	P	P
U	U	L	M	M	P	P	P	L
P	P	P	L	P	P	L	P	L
L	L	U	P	P	M	U	M	L
M	L	U	L	L	U	U	P	L
P	P	L	P	P	U	M	M	P
L	L	P	M	M	L	M	P	P
L	M	P	M	L	U	M	U	P

Find the word 'plum' in the grid. It may be hidden horizontally, vertically or diagonally.

CROSSWORD

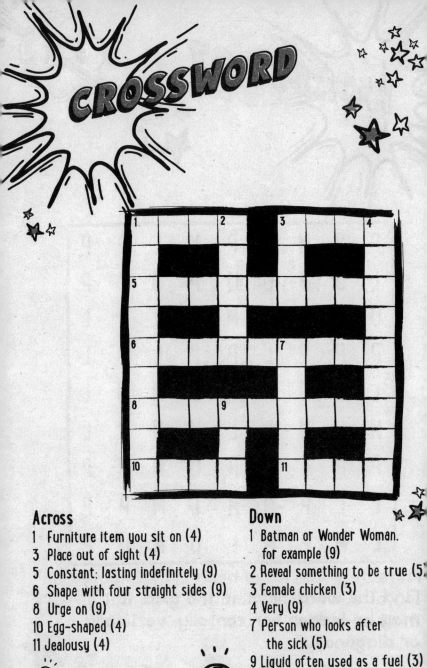

Across

1 Furniture item you sit on (4)
3 Place out of sight (4)
5 Constant; lasting indefinitely (9)
6 Shape with four straight sides (9)
8 Urge on (9)
10 Egg-shaped (4)
11 Jealousy (4)

Down

1 Batman or Wonder Woman, for example (9)
2 Reveal something to be true (5)
3 Female chicken (3)
4 Very (9)
7 Person who looks after the sick (5)
9 Liquid often used as a fuel (3)

WORD ILLUSION

BLHAICTE

ABRRAVE

BLHARP

Pairs of words have been superimposed on top of each other. Can you work out what the words are?

BREAK THE CODE

DIFTUOVU =

CFFDI =

TZDBNPSF =

Each of these trees has had each letter replaced by the letter before it in the alphabet (so 'B' becomes 'A' and so on). Can you break the code to reveal the answers?

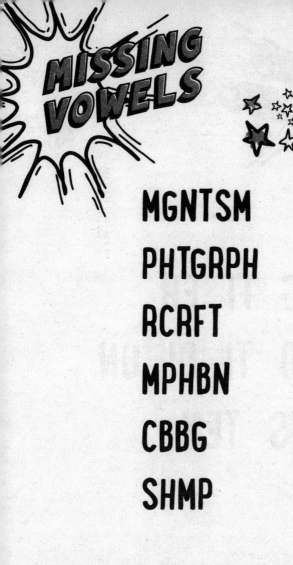

MISSING VOWELS

MGNTSM

PHTGRPH

RCRFT

MPHBN

CBBG

SHMP

These six words have had their vowels removed. Can you add them back in to find the words?

WORD SPLITS

NG FI ER

AD TI DI ON

NIS TEN

These three words have been split into
smaller sections and shuffled around.
Can you put them back in order?

WORDFINDER

M	W	O	C	G
X	C	Y	R	E
S	A	W	S	K
O	F	K	T	X
B	M	Y	F	B

A word has been hidden in the letter grid above. Simply cross out any letter that appears more than once and the hidden word will reveal itself. If you'd like an added challenge, see if you can solve the puzzle in your head without crossing any letters out.

WORD LADDER

FARM
HENS

Move from the word at the top of the ladder to the word at the bottom of the ladder by changing one letter on each step of the ladder to form a new word. Do not rearrange the order of the letters.

(Note that there may be more than one way to solve the puzzle. Word ladders often have multiple solutions.)

ANAGRAM CONNECT

Follow the line from each letter at the top and write that letter in the empty circle it is connected to. These letters will spell out the answer word.

WORDSEARCH

Find each of the words in the grid. Words may be hidden horizontally, vertically or diagonally.

```
O B I O L O G Y H E O P A
C H E M I S T R Y N T F G
H B K R M J G E R M A N E
M E D I A S T U D I E S O
M H F L T E S W L C D M G
B T R R H A N P S E R Y R
O A E A E G P G A G U R A
Z R L W M N E A L N Q C P
D T I U A O C L A I I K H
R R G B T L B H W L S S Y
A O I F I T A L I A N H H
M R O F C G I C M U S I C
A S N R S H I S T O R Y M
```

ART	FRENCH	MATHEMATICS
BIOLOGY	GEOGRAPHY	MEDIA STUDIES
CHEMISTRY	GERMAN	MUSIC
DRAMA	HISTORY	RELIGION
ENGLISH	ITALIAN	SPANISH

CODEBREAKER

VDKK CNMD, SGHR OTYYKD HR
RNKUDC!

Can you work out what you must do to
each letter above in order to crack the
code and spell out the answer message?

FOLDED PAPER

MACHINE

ORANGE

PORTRAIT

Three pieces of paper have been folded in half. They each have a word on - can you work out what those words are?

ANAGRAMS

A NEW HELLO

HUGE ROBIN

FROG FLUTE

MIGHT EARN

REACH CART

HOT TEAPOTS

Can you rearrange the scrambled letters above to reveal six new words?

ANAGRAM CONNECT

Follow the line from each letter at the top and write that letter in the empty circle it is connected to. These letters will spell out the answer word.

WORDWHEEL

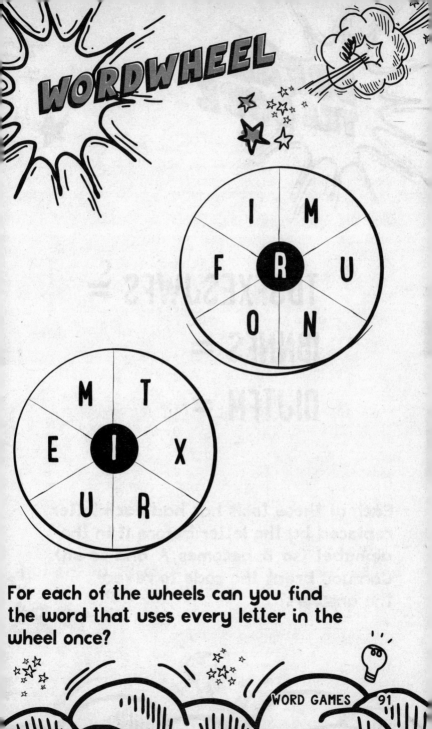

For each of the wheels can you find the word that uses every letter in the wheel once?

BREAK THE CODE

TDSFXESJWFS =
IBNNFS =
DIJTFM =

Each of these tools has had each letter replaced by the letter before it in the alphabet (so 'B' becomes 'A' and so on). Can you break the code to reveal the answers?

WORD LADDER

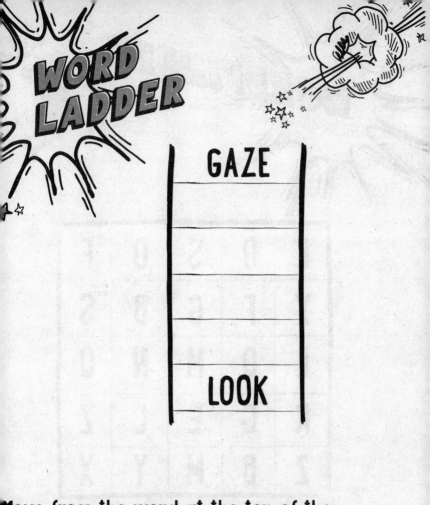

GAZE

LOOK

Move from the word at the top of the ladder to the word at the bottom of the ladder by changing one letter on each step of the ladder to form a new word. Do not rearrange the order of the letters.

(Note that there may be more than one way to solve the puzzle. Word ladders often have multiple solutions.)

WORDFINDER

L	D	S	O	F
X	F	G	B	S
L	Q	M	N	Q
K	G	E	L	Z
Z	B	M	Y	X

A word has been hidden in the letter grid above. Simply cross out any letter that appears more than once and the hidden word will reveal itself. If you'd like an added challenge, see if you can solve the puzzle in your head without crossing any letters out.

CODEBREAKER

D	C	H	A	F	F	I	N	C	H
T	U	R	K	E	Y	G	I	H	O
L	C	C	D	V	R	O	B	I	N
E	K	N	K	U	S	M	I	C	T
D	O	V	E	L	W	A	S	K	H
C	O	O	T	T	A	G	W	E	R
C	R	O	W	U	L	P	A	N	U
E	S	T	A	R	L	I	N	G	S
G	O	O	S	E	O	E	A	G	H
H	A	W	K	L	W	R	E	N	E

CHAFFINCH MAGPIE
CHICKEN ROBIN
COOT STARLING
CROW SWALLOW
CUCKOO SWAN
DOVE THRUSH
DUCK TURKEY
GOOSE VULTURE
HAWK WREN
IBIS

Find all the birds in the grid. Words
may be hidden horizontally, vertically
or diagonally. Once you have found all
the words, can you find the name of
another bird in the grid with the letters
that are left?

KRISS KROSS

Place all the words into the grid once each to complete the puzzle.

3 letters
SKY
SUN

4 letters
MOON

5 letters
COMET
ORBIT

6 letters
GALAXY
METEOR
NEBULA
PLANET

8 letters
ASTEROID
UNIVERSE

9 letters
ASTRONOMY
SUPERNOVA
TELESCOPE

10 letters
ATMOSPHERE

ANAGRAM CONNECT

S A I L E D

Follow the line from each letter at the top and write that letter in the empty circle it is connected to. These letters will spell out the answer word.

MISSING VOWELS

LNGG

MRGNCY

TLPHN

PNPPL

BGNNNG

GRSSHPPR

These six words have had their vowels removed. Can you add them back in to find the words?

WORDSPOT

Find the word 'bird' in the grid. It may be hidden horizontally, vertically or diagonally.

D	B	B	D	D	B	R	B	B	D
B	R	I	D	B	I	R	R	B	R
R	R	R	I	B	I	B	D	D	B
D	R	R	B	B	D	B	D	I	R
D	I	D	I	B	D	R	I	D	D
R	I	B	R	I	I	D	B	R	D
R	I	B	R	I	D	B	R	D
B	I	R	I	I	B	B	I	B	D
I	R	I	R	R	B	B	R	B
I	I	B	B	I	B	D	B	R	D

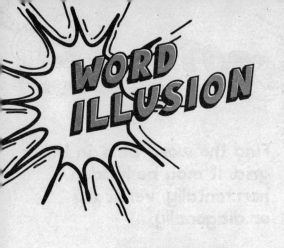

WORD ILLUSION

E OSE

DAUNBY

BORBOW

Pairs of words have been superimposed on top of each other. Can you work out what the words are?

WORD SPLITS

BI GY OLO

OW YE LL

AH CHE ET

These three words have been split into smaller sections and shuffled around. Can you put them back in order?

WORDWHEEL

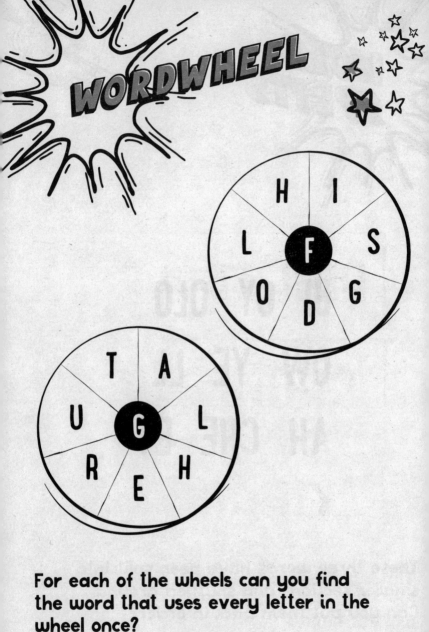

For each of the wheels can you find the word that uses every letter in the wheel once?

FOLDED PAPER

PINEAPPLE

SHOULDER

KINGDOM

Three pieces of paper have been folded in half. They each have a word on - can you work out what those words are?

ANAGRAM CONNECT

M E T E O R

Follow the line from each letter at the top and write that letter in the empty circle it is connected to. These letters will spell out the answer word.

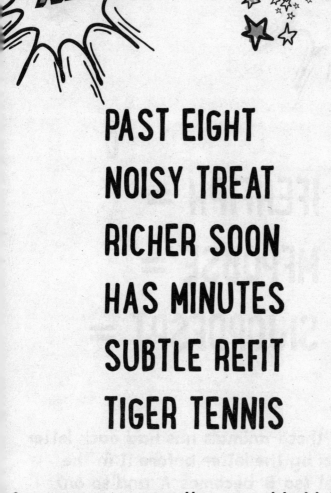

ANAGRAMS

PAST EIGHT

NOISY TREAT

RICHER SOON

HAS MINUTES

SUBTLE REFIT

TIGER TENNIS

Can you rearrange the scrambled letters to reveal six new words?

CODEBREAKER

IFEHFIPH =

MFPQBSE =

SIJOPDFSPT =

Each of these animals has had each letter replaced by the letter before it in the alphabet (so 'B' becomes 'A' and so on). Can you break the code to reveal the answers?

CROSSWORD

Across

4 Run quickly (of a horse) (6)
6 Join together (4)
7 Shade of a colour (3)
8 Popular edible fish (4)
9 Opposite of home (4)
10 Form of public transport (3)
11 One more than four (4)
12 Sport played by Emma Raducanu (6)

Down

1 Best-loved (9)
2 The letters we use when writing (8)
3 Impressive or incredible (9)
5 Nice (8)

WORDSEARCH

Find each of the words in the grid. Words may be hidden horizontally or vertically.

```
O M N S A U S A G E O P
L U Y T A Q P R S X N I
I S W L W E T Z A N N N
V H B L X U P V N S O E
E R L B H A P R M P N A
M O Z Z E R E L L A S P
I O N S M R R W Q R P P
K M A N C H O V Y A I L
T O M A T O N O Q G N E
S A L A M I I I E U A G
V C H I C K E N E S C D
U R I C O T T A R N H U
```

ANCHOVY   HAM   OLIVE   PINEAPPLE   SAUSAGE

ASPARAGUS   MOZZARELLA   ONION   RICOTTA   SPINACH

CHICKEN   MUSHROOM   PEPPERONI   SALAMI   TOMATO

BREAK THE CODE

PBATENGHYNGVBAF LBH UNIR FBYIRQ
GUR SVANY PBQR CHMMYR VA GUVF
OBBX

**Here is a tricky code for you to crack —
can you reveal its contents?**

Hint: you need to shift each letter up or down the alphabet
(it doesn't matter which) by the same amount.

KRISS KROSS

Place all the words into the grid once each to complete the puzzle.

4 letters
GOLF
SUMO

6 letters
KARATE
ROWING
SKIING
TENNIS

7 letters
CYCLING
RUNNING
SAILING
SURFING

9 letters
BADMINTON

10 letters
BASKETBALL

12 letters
SNOWBOARDIN[G]

WORD LADDER

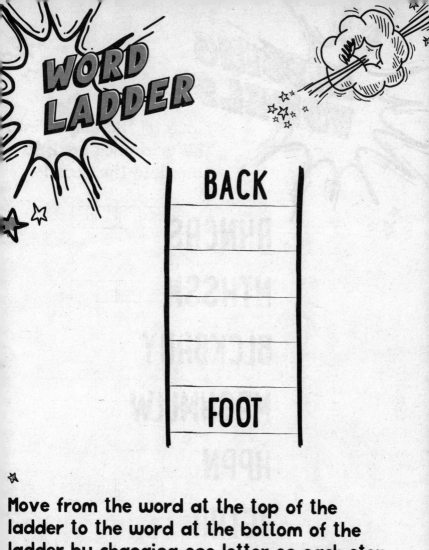

BACK

FOOT

Move from the word at the top of the ladder to the word at the bottom of the ladder by changing one letter on each step of the ladder to form a new word. Do not rearrange the order of the letters.

(Note that there may be more than one way to solve the puzzle. Word ladders often have multiple solutions.)

MISSING VOWELS

RHNCRS

NTHSSM

BLCKBRRY

MRSHMLLW

HPPN

TGTHR

These six words have had their vowels removed. Can you add them back in to find the words?

FOLDED PAPER

SPRING

WEDNESDAY

WEEKEND

Three pieces of paper have been folded in half. They each have a word on – can you work out what those words are?

WORDWHEEL

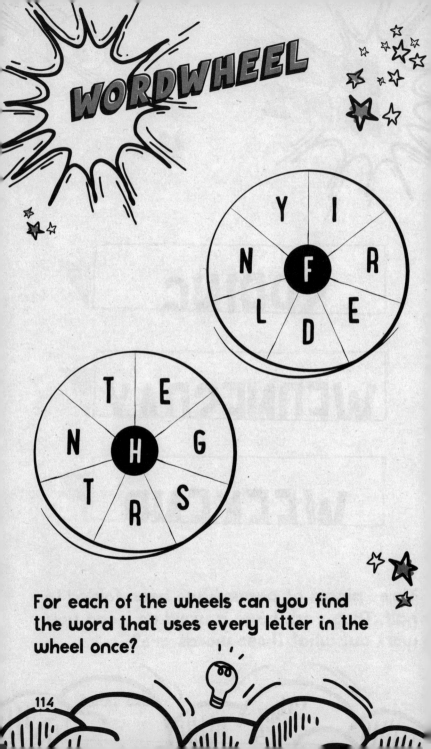

For each of the wheels can you find the word that uses every letter in the wheel once?

114

WORD ILLUSION

GAVKEE

ERAVE

HEGNY

Pairs of words have been superimposed on top of each other. Can you work out what the words are?

WORDFINDER

I	W	U	N	X
B	L	N	J	A
Y	B	C	I	N
X	Z	K	Z	U
Y	W	L	E	T

A word has been hidden in the letter grid above. Simply cross out any letter that appears more than once and the hidden word will reveal itself. If you'd like an added challenge, see if you can solve the puzzle in your head without crossing any letters out.

WORDSEARCH

Find each of the words in the grid. Words may be hidden horizontally, vertically or diagonally and in either a forwards or backwards direction.

```
O U T D O O R S K G P W R S
H G T P C R G N I K I H T U
N A L A Y N R Z O E M R R T
R B I R D N R E T N A L E A
T G E K L G C U R X N D M O
A N E P X E U L D E O T M C
G I X R I I G Q I O Q E U N
W P R T I C N N T M E V S I
A E E E R F N N I Z B S Y A
T E G N I A L I Y H S I R R
E L K T L A I C C V S C N O
R S O A K L A R L L I I R G
S T O O B R R T L L K T F M
T W I L D E R N E S S V V L
```

BOOTS	LANTERN	SLEEPING BAG
CLIMBING	OUTDOORS	SUMMER
FIRE	PARK	TENT
FISHING	PICNIC	WATER
HIKING	RAINCOAT	WILDERNESS

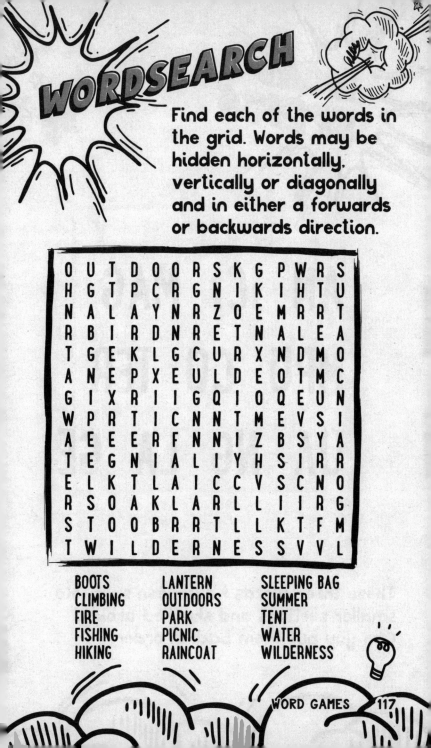

AN ICI MAG

MPU CO TER

UA NG LA GE

These three words have been split into smaller sections and shuffled around. Can you put them back in order?

WORDWHEEL

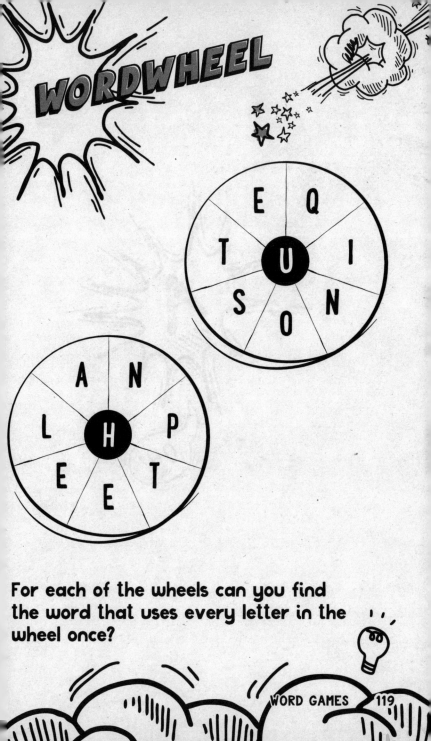

For each of the wheels can you find the word that uses every letter in the wheel once?

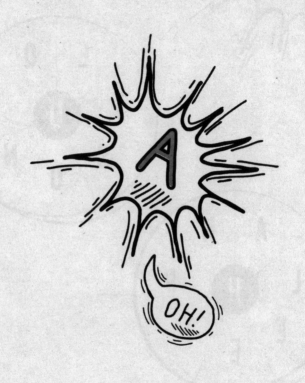

Page 4 – Folded paper

COUNTRY
MOUNTAIN
BIRTHDAY

Page 5 – Wordspot

A	P	A	P	A	P
P	A	L	A	A	E
P	L	E	P	A	A
L	L	P	P	L	E
P	A	L	L	L	P
E	P	A	E	P	L

Page 6 – Word ladder

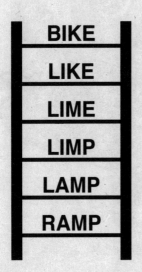

BIKE
LIKE
LIME
LIMP
LAMP
RAMP

Page 7 – Missing vowels

SWIMMING
TRAVELLING
CALCULATOR
EIGHTEEN
MARATHON
UMBRELLA

Page 8 – Wordfinder

GAME

Page 9 – Word illusion

FAST SLOW
HARD EASY
REAL FAKE

Page 10 – Break the code

PAPER
CRAYON
RULER

Page 11 – Wordwheel

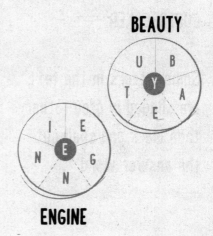

BEAUTY

ENGINE

Page 12 – Kriss kross

Page 13 – Word splits

SAFETY

CINEMA

EASTER

Page 14 – Codebreaker

CODEBREAKER

Some letters in the text are shaded in grey rather than black and spell out the answer word.

Page 15 – Anagram connect

Page 16 - Anagrams	Page 17 - Folded paper
DOUBLE	PATIENT
TADPOLE	CREATIVE
PLASTIC	ADDITION
REPTILE	
HAMSTER	
AIRPORT	

Page 18 - Wordwheel

CAMERA

LIQUID

Page 19 - Wordfinder

CAKE

Page 20 – Wordsearch

```
P T L A U G H T E R A D
L P B A L L O O N S F R
F A M I L Y P B W X J I
F C E L E B R A T I O N
R C A N D L E S K C M K
I Z R Y B A S V F A U S
E A K L H I E C O K S H
N D A N C I N G O E I I
D T O X S P T R D R C O
S Z A S Z U S G A M E S
O L G S U R P R I S E R
P A R T Y H A T S S F G
```

Page 21 – Word ladder

READ

BEAD

BEAT

BOAT

BOOT

BOOK

Page 22 – Wordfinder

TUNA

Page 23 – Codebreaker

SECRET
The missing letters spell
the answer word
SADNESS
ECLIPSE
COMIC
REGISTER
ENTRANCE
TALENT

Page 24 – Word splits

TIMETABLE
DANCING
CASTLE

Page 25 – Crossword

M	A	R	S		H	E	R	O
Y		E		O			M
S	I	G	N	A	T	U	R	E
T		S					L
E	X	P	E	N	S	I	V	E
R				Y			T
I	N	C	O	R	R	E	C	T
E		A		U			E
S	T	A	R		P	L	U	S

Page 26 – Folded paper

REVEAL
WINDOW
CAPTAIN

Page 27 – Anagram connect

Page 28 – Missing vowels

ENVIRONMENT
WONDERFUL
DOUGHNUT
COMEDIAN
MOTORBIKE
NONSENSE

Page 29 – Wordwheel

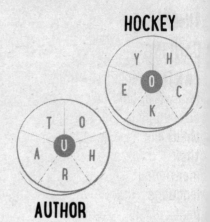

HOCKEY

AUTHOR

Page 30 – Word illusion

WEST   EAST

HARD   SOFT

HIGH   DEEP

Page 31 – Break the code

ORANGE
PURPLE
YELLOW

Page 32 – Codebreaker

ENGLISH.

Some of the words in the paragraph have letters missing: adding them back in (shown in bold below) spells out 'English'. Did you spot them all?

th**e**ir
me**n**tioned
lan**g**uages
particu**l**arly
th**i**s
succe**s**sfully
sc**h**ool

Page 33 – Wordspot

S	O	H	R	R	S	H
O	O	S	R	E	O	O
S	R	O	E	E	O	R
O	S	E	E	S	S	S
E	H	O	H	R	H	E
E	S	S	S	R	H	H
R	H	R	H	S	E	S

Page 34 – Crossword

Page 35 – Wordfinder

YEAR

Page 36 – Word ladder

BIRD
BIND
BEND
BENT
BEST
NEST

Page 37 – Anagrams

MUSEUM
WHISTLE
FOOTBALL
PORPOISE
MEDICINE
LEMONADE

Page 38 – Wordwheel

BONFIRE

F E
O N R
B I

SPARKLE

P E
L K A
S R

Page 39 – Anagram connect

E D I T S

T I D E S

Page 40 – Wordsearch

```
M O N G O L I A P S I A
C H I N A I N D I A T R
T I Z C U N E B P J T G
W A E P S D Z R O A E E
U M U O T O L A L P R N
I Z I R R N U Z A R J T
E I N T A E F I N M I N
A T L U L S P L D X Z N
E A V G I I C A N A D A
P L E A A M E X I C O
J Y T L S R U S S I A T
B W A L G E R I A E O Z
```

Page 41 – Kriss kross

```
E C S T A T I C            S
              H        O    U
    S       G R I N N I N G
  S M I L I N G  I      T    N
              I        E    N
              L        N    Y
G L E E F U L          T
  M       I    E        D    C
  I       G    D             A
  N       H    M    J        R
  G       T    E    J O Y F U L
          T    R    L        R
  C H E E R F U L   L        E
          D    Y    Y        E
```

Page 42 – Wordfinder

FIELD

Page 43 – Codebreaker

All the vowels have been removed from the sentence. Adding these back in reveals the sentence: SURPRISINGLY IT IS POSSIBLE FOR THE HUMAN BRAIN TO WORK OUT THE CONTENTS OF SENTENCES EVEN WHEN ALL THE VOWELS HAVE BEEN REMOVED FROM THEM. AS YOU HAVE JUST DEMONSTRATED.

Page 44 – Anagrams

BEYOND
SKELETON
SNOWFLAKE
PASSENGER
SUBMARINE
YESTERDAY

Page 45 – Folded paper

TICKET
ADVENTURE
DRAWING

Page 46 – Anagram connect

H O R S E

S H O R E

Page 47 – Word splits

ANIMATE
GRAVITY
PERFECT

Page 48 – Codebreaker

The first letter of the first flower, the second letter of the second flower and so on spell out the answer word CROCUS on the diagonal:

CLOVER
ORCHID
SNOWDROP
HYACINTH
NASTURTIUM
NARCISSUS

Page 49 – Wordwheel

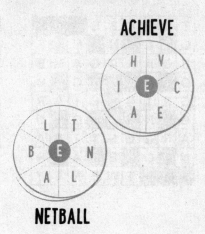

ACHIEVE

NETBALL

Page 50 – Folded paper

VEGETABLE
EXPLORE
BOOKSHELF

Page 51 – Word illusion

COOL WARM

MEAN KIND

DEVIL ANGEL

Page 52 – Crossword

Page 53 – Missing vowels

PICTURE

DIFFICULTY

TEMPERATURE

DEFINITION

PARSNIP

DIRECTION

Page 54 – Break the code

CLOWN

JUGGLER

ACROBAT

Page 55 – Wordfinder

CREAM

Page 56 – Wordwheel   Page 57 – Wordspot

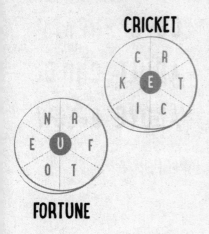

CRICKET

FORTUNE

S	U	S	E	S	U	U	S
M	E	O	U	S	O	E	U
U	M	S	M	E	M	M	O
U	O	S	O	U	S	S	M
M	U	S	E	U	S	U	S
S	S	O	E	O	M	M	O
E	E	S	E	O	E	M	U
E	U	S	M	S	O	M	M

Page 58 – Word splits   Page 59 – Codebreaker

COMPASS   APPLE
SPARKLE
WEEKEND

Page 60 – Wordsearch

Page 61 – Word illusion

COLD   HEAT

ADULT   CHILD

ABOVE   BELOW

Page 62 – Folded paper

ALLIGATOR
DIAMOND
BLACKBIRD

Page 63 – Break the code

CLOUD
HURRICANE
THUNDER

Page 64 – Missing vowels

PORCUPINE
MARMALADE
SOMETIMES
CUCUMBER
FORTNIGHT
WARDROBE

Page 65 – Wordfinder

BREAD

Page 66 – Anagram connect

Page 67 – Word ladder

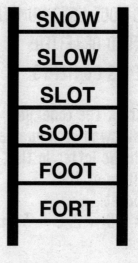

Page 68 – Kriss kross

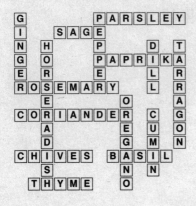

Page 69 – Wordwheel

RAINBOW

QUARTER

Page 70 – Codebreaker

THIS CODE USES NUMBERS INSTEAD OF LETTERS TO HIDE ITS CONTENTS.

To crack the code, you must swap each number with the letter in that position of the alphabet:
A = 1, B = 2, C = 3 and so on.

Page 71 – Word splits

FURNITURE

READING

BREAKFAST

Page 72 – Wordfinder

EARTH

Page 73 – Anagram connect

Page 74 – Wordwheel

JOURNEY

RECEIPT

Page 75 – Folded paper

ENJOYMENT
FOOTBALL
ENORMOUS

Page 76 – Anagrams

ANTELOPE
TEMPORARY
ADVANTAGE
ALBATROSS
AEROPLANE
VEGETABLE

Page 77 – Wordspot

P	P	M	P	P	M	L	P	P
L	U	P	U	U	P	U	P	P
U	U	L	M	M	P	P	P	L
P	P	P	L	P	P	L	P	L
L	L	U	P	P	M	U	M	L
M	L	U	L	L	U	U	P	L
P	P	L	P	P	U	M	M	P
L	L	P	M	M	L	M	P	P
L	M	P	M	L	U	M	U	P

Page 78 – Crossword

S	O	F	A		H	I	D	E
U			D		E			X
P	E	R	M	A	N	E	N	T
E			I					R
R	E	C	T	A	N	G	L	E
H			U					M
E	N	C	O	U	R	A	G	E
R			I		S			L
O	V	A	L		E	N	V	Y

Page 79 – Word illusion

WHITE BLACK
ARRIVE DEPART
BLUNT SHARP

Page 80 – Break the code

CHESTNUT
BEECH
SYCAMORE

Page 81 – Missing vowels

MAGNETISM
PHOTOGRAPH
AIRCRAFT
AMPHIBIAN
CABBAGE
SHAMPOO

Page 82 – Word splits

FINGER
ADDITION
TENNIS

Page 83 – Wordfinder

GREAT

Page 84 – Word ladder

FARM

HARM

HARD

HERD

HERS

HENS

Page 85 – Anagram connect

R E S C U E

S E C U R E

Page 86 – Wordsearch

Page 87 – Codebreaker

You must replace each letter with the one that comes after it in the alphabet. for instance V becomes W and D becomes E to spell out the answer message:

WELL DONE. THIS PUZZLE IS SOLVED!

Page 88 – Folded paper

MACHINE
ORANGE
PORTRAIT

Page 89 – Anagrams

HALLOWEEN
NEIGHBOUR
FORGETFUL
NIGHTMARE
CHARACTER
TOOTHPASTE

Page 90 – Anagram connect

FOREST

SOFTER

Page 91 – Wordwheel

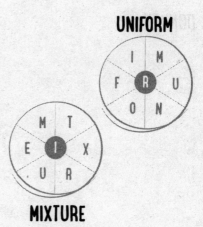

UNIFORM

MIXTURE

Page 92 – Break the code

SCREWDRIVER
HAMMER
CHISEL

Page 93 – Word ladder

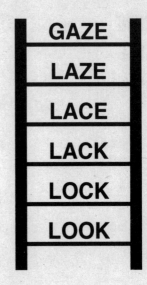

GAZE
LAZE
LACE
LACK
LOCK
LOOK

Page 94 – Wordfinder

DONKEY

Page 95 – Codebreaker

Hidden bird: GOLDEN EAGLE

Page 96 – Kriss kross

Page 97 – Anagram connect

Page 98 – Missing vowels

LANGUAGE

EMERGENCY

TELEPHONE

PINEAPPLE

BEGINNING

GRASSHOPPER

Page 99 – Wordspot

D	B	B	D	D	B	R	B	B	D
B	R	I	D	B	I	R	R	B	R
R	R	R	I	B	I	B	D	D	B
D	R	R	B	B	D	B	D	I	R
D	I	D	I	B	D	R	I	D	D
R	I	B	R	I	I	D	B	R	I
R	R	I	B	R	I	D	B	R	D
B	I	R	I	I	B	B	I	B	D
I	R	I	R	R	B	B	B	R	B
I	I	B	B	I	B	D	B	R	D

Page 100 – Word illusion

LOSE   FIND

DAINTY CLUMSY

BORROW RETURN

Page 101 – Word splits

BIOLOGY
YELLOW
CHEETAH

Page 102 – Wordwheel

GOLDFISH

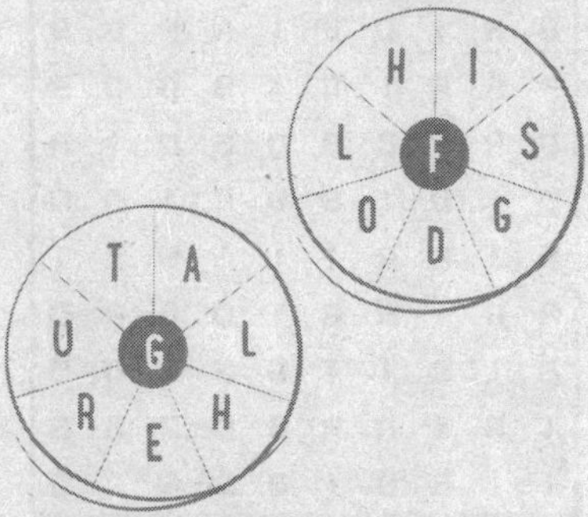

LAUGHTER

Page 103 – Folded paper

PINEAPPLE
SHOULDER
KINGDOM

Page 104 - Anagram connect

M E T E O R

R E M O T E

Page 105 - Anagrams

SPAGHETTI
STATIONERY
RHINOCEROS
ENTHUSIASM
BUTTERFLIES
INTERESTING

Page 106 - Codebreaker

HEDGEHOG
LEOPARD
RHINOCEROS

Page 107 - Crossword

Page 108 – Wordsearch

Page 109 – Break the code

You must shift each letter up (or down) the alphabet 13 positions in order to crack the code. therefore P becomes C. B becomes O. and so on.
This reveals the answer:

CONGRATULATIONS YOU HAVE SOLVED THE FINAL CODE PUZZLE IN THIS BOOK.

Page 110 – Kriss kross

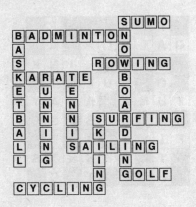

Page 111 – Word ladder

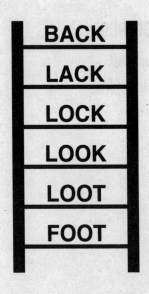

Page 112 – Missing vowels

RHINOCEROS
ENTHUSIASM
BLACKBERRY
MARSHMALLOW
HAPPEN
TOGETHER

Page 113 – Folded paper

SPRING
WEDNESDAY
WEEKEND

Page 114 – Wordwheel

FRIENDLY

STRENGTH

Page 115 – Word illusion

TAKE   GIVE

LEAVE   ENTER

LIGHT   HEAVY

Page 116 – Wordfinder

JACKET

Page 117 – Wordsearch

Page 118 – Word splits

MAGICIAN
COMPUTER
LANGUAGE

Page 119 – Wordwheel

QUESTION

ELEPHANT

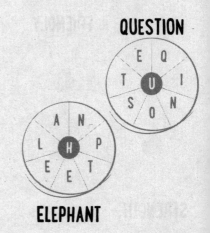

NOTES

NOTES

NOTES

NOTES